W9-ABK-035

YOU'RE IN BUSINESS!

GET A JOB

MAKING STUFF TO SELL

Ryan Jacobson

Illustrations by Jon Cannell

$1.79

Lerner Publications Company • Minneapolis

For my brother Jason and our neighbor
Paul, co-owners of my first lemonade
stand —R.J.

To Ramone Munoz, for your dedication and
passion to teaching —J.C.

Text and illustrations copyright © 2015 by Lerner Publishing
Group, Inc.

All rights reserved. International copyright secured. No part
of this book may be reproduced, stored in a retrieval system,
or transmitted in any form or by any means—electronic,
mechanical, photocopying, recording, or otherwise—without
the prior written permission of Lerner Publishing Group,
Inc., except for the inclusion of brief quotations in an
acknowledged review.

Lerner Publications Company
A division of Lerner Publishing Group, Inc.
241 First Avenue North
Minneapolis, MN 55401 USA

For reading levels and more information, look up this title
at www.lernerbooks.com.

Library of Congress Cataloging-in-Publication Data

Jacobson, Ryan.
    Get a job making stuff to sell / by Ryan Jacobson ;
  illustrated by Jon Cannell.
      pages   cm. — (You're in business!)
    Includes index.
    ISBN 978-1-4677-3837-8 (lib. bdg. : alk. paper)
    ISBN 978-1-4677-4757-8 (eBook)
    1. Moneymaking projects for children—Juvenile
  literature. 2. Selling—Handicraft—Juvenile literature.
  3. Entrepreneurship—Juvenile literature. I. Cannell, Jon,
  illustrator. II. Title.
  HF5392.J364 2015
  331.702—dc23   2013044296

Manufactured in the United States of America
1 - CG - 7/15/14

TABLE OF CONTENTS

GO
TEAM

INTRODUCTION:

TURN YOUR

TALENT INTO CASH!

You have talent. Maybe you don't think of yourself as super creative or amazingly crafty. But you've probably made something that gave you a sense of pride. It might've been an assignment or a gift for someone. Or perhaps it was just a fun activity for you. You devoted some time, effort, and thought to the project, and it turned out well. More important, you enjoyed creating it.

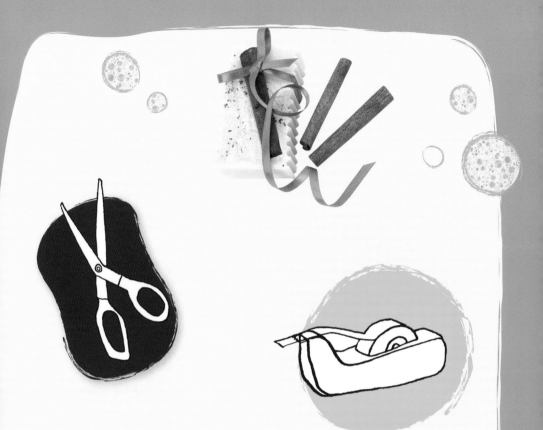

What if you could use your talent not just to feel great but to earn cash? It sounds like a dream, but it isn't. With the right planning and a smart approach, you can turn your skills into a moneymaking business!

It doesn't matter how old you are or what your talent is. If you make something that's high quality, people will buy it. If you can invest a little bit of money, you can make hundreds of dollars in profit! And best of all, you'll have fun doing it.

LEMONADE STAND...

Selling lemonade is one of the oldest businesses for young people. Perhaps you tried it when you were younger. You made a pitcher of lemonade, set up a stand in front of your home, and sold a few cups to the people who stopped. Of course, you probably only earned a few bucks, and you might have drunk more than you sold! But even if your childhood lemonade stand didn't bring in much cash, you can set up a stand that will. You'll just need to take a more grown-up approach.

First, choose a time and a place where a lot of people—better yet, a lot of thirsty people—will be. If plenty of people walk and drive past your home, then the driveway, the front yard, or the sidewalk could be a good place to start. Or you can go into business with a friend who lives in a better location. Other promising spots include a beach, a park, and outside a shopping center. Talk to your family about where you can set up. You may need to get special permission to be there. You may also need to pay certain fees to your city or state.

If you're in a good area and it's the right time of day, you'll see many people. Every one of them is a potential customer. But how do you get them to stop? First and foremost, make sure that you're selling a good product. Your lemonade needs to taste delicious. You can use instant mixes, and none of your customers will complain. But if you really want to wow them, make freshly squeezed lemonade. It costs a little more to create, but your customers will also be willing to pay more for it. Here's a simple recipe:

2 cups freshly squeezed lemon juice (5 to 6 lemons)
1 to 2 cups sugar (depending on how sweet you want your lemonade)
12 cups water

Mix these ingredients, serve the finished product in a glass full of ice, and trust that your customers will come back for more! Once you're off to a solid start, you may want to experiment with different lemonade flavors, such as raspberry or ginger. Some variety will make your stand unique and help it appeal to even more customers.

Working Wisdom: Make It a Fund-Raiser

In 2000 a four-year-old cancer patient named Alexandra (Alex) Scott started a lemonade stand. She wanted to raise money for the fight against childhood cancer. That little stand grew into Alex's Lemonade Stand Foundation, which has raised more than $65 million! You can make a difference in the world—and draw attention to your business—by donating a share of your profits to a charitable cause.

You'll have to buy the ingredients, so decide how much you're willing to invest up front. You can start small and blend your recipe only two or three times. Then buy more ingredients with your profits. But remember that you'll need to buy ice and cups too. You'll also want a cooler to store your ice.

Keep track of all your expenses. Figure out your unit cost, or how much a single glass of lemonade costs to make. With the recipe you use, how many cups can you fill before the lemonade is gone? If the supplies and ingredients cost ten dollars and if they fill twenty cups, then each glass costs you fifty cents.

Knowing this will help you determine your price. At that rate, if you charge only twenty-five cents per cup, you'll be losing money! Since you want to *make* money, you need to charge more than fifty cents. How much more? That depends on what your customers are willing to pay. It's best to start low. You can always raise your price as the lemonade gets more popular.

Working Wisdom: Business Basics

To set a course for success, ask yourself the basic business questions: what, who, why, where, when, and how.

What will you sell?

Who will buy it?

Why will people buy it?

Where and *when* should (and can) you sell it?

How will you stand out from your competition?

When you set up your lemonade stand, make sure it looks like a well-run business. Keep your booth clean and neatly organized. Put a lid on your lemonade pitcher or cover it with a paper towel to keep bugs out. You might even want to put hand sanitizer on the table to show that you care about cleanliness. If you're using a card table, cover it with a bright tablecloth. Display a big, readable sign that states what you're selling and how much it costs. If you're in a good spot, if your price is fair, and if your lemonade is tasty, it will be in demand!

BAKE SALE

Do you have a passion for making delicious food? Or maybe you just want to add something extra to your lemonade stand. Either way, here's a business idea for you: a bake sale! Turn your skill in the kitchen into money by preparing a few different kinds of desserts. If they look good, taste good, and are priced right, those desserts could bring you a profit.

You can focus on one type of dessert or offer a variety. But keep your selection to five or fewer different treats. It will save you a lot of work and will make it easier for your customers to choose what they want. If you've only mastered one or two baked goods, don't worry. You can fill out your selection with custom-made snack mixes. Create unique combinations of pretzels, nuts, pieces of candy, and dried fruit. Look online for snack mix recipes that use spices or syrupy coatings. Then put your own spin on those recipes with ingredients you can get easily and cheaply.

It's smart to include healthful options among your bake sale items. Look for recipes that feature fruit or nuts. (Trail mix can have both!)

Even when it comes to the sweet stuff, many recipes cut down on sugar and butter—or replace them with other ingredients—without losing the tastiness.

Once you've finalized your menu, figure out where you'll sell your products. You can start with a table in your driveway. But baked goods are easy to transport, so you have other options too. Maybe you can sell at a local sporting event, at your place of worship, or at a community celebration. How about setting up at your neighbors' garage sales? When you come up with a good place for your bake sale, make sure you get permission to be there. Then find out exactly how much space you'll have. It might be a whole room or just one corner. Your venue will probably have a spare table and a trash can you can use for your booth. If so, ask to see the table beforehand so you know how big it is. If there isn't an extra table on-site, you'll need to bring a card table or two.

Next, advertise your bake sale. Send invitations to family, friends, and classmates about two weeks before the sale. See if you can get your local newspaper to write a story about it. (If you strike out, you can place a paid ad.) With permission, post flyers near your bake sale location, in local businesses, and in public places. If your bake sale is tied to another event, ask if you can get a brief mention in that event's publicity.

Then it's time to go shopping. Make a list of ingredients you'll need for your baked goods. Head to the store to buy anything you don't already have. While you're at it, pick up the other supplies you'll need: sturdy paper plates, napkins, resealable plastic bags or plastic wrap to hold your desserts, and perhaps a colorful plastic tablecloth. If you want to get fancy, choose colorful patterned plates and add some ribbon to your shopping cart. You'll also need poster board or a large, sturdy sheet of paper for a sign.

A day or two before the sale, begin baking. You want your products to be as fresh as possible, so don't start too far in advance. But make sure you give yourself enough time to finish before the event. While you're baking, have a trusted adult supervise and offer suggestions. You might want to include a friend too. After all, baking is more fun with company!

When the food is ready, your last step is to package it. Carefully cut any brownies or cakes so that every piece is about the same size. Divide your portions of snack mix evenly too. Use the serving-size instructions on recipes as a guide for making portions. Then mix and match your desserts into a variety of sizes and prices. You can sell individual servings, plates heaping with goodies, and everything in between. Slide each plate into a plastic bag or wrap it in plastic. Then put a price on everything. You can make price tags out of paper and string. A neatly ripped piece of tape and a permanent marker will also do the trick. For an extra decorative touch, seal your bags with ribbons.

On the day of your event, arrive about half an hour early to set up. Bring napkins, extra plastic wrap, shopping bags, and a small box or bag of cash. When arranging your desserts, remember that some customers may have food allergies. For instance, you may want to

keep foods containing peanuts or peanut butter separate from your other offerings, or at least mark them clearly. And keep your lists of ingredients handy, in case anyone wants to know what's in a recipe. If you have food to spare, offer free bite-sized samples. Be polite, thank people for coming, and let them leave with a good impression of you. With any luck, they'll come back again next time.

Working Wisdom: Keeping Track of Cash

Whenever you sell a product, you'll need somewhere to store your earnings as people pay you. Have a small box or zip-up pouch to hold cash. Before you start your sale, put some coins and small bills in your money holder so that you can make change for your earliest customers. When you give someone change for a large bill, count it out loud as you give it to the person to show you've done your math right. At the end of your sale, count how much money you've got (minus what you originally brought along for making change). Keep a record of your profits from each event.

SOAP

Bake sales and lemonade stands are about selling things people want. But there are some things that people need—like soap. It may not sound like an exciting product, but you can make homemade soap that's unique and appealing. People have to buy their soap somewhere—why not from you?

Soapmaking involves some up-front expenses. You need to buy at least one plastic soap mold. You can find molds online if no nearby stores stock them. (Plastic cups work too.) You'll also need cooking spray, plastic wrap, a microwave-safe liquid measuring cup, and Popsicle sticks. Visit a craft store to get glycerin soap. You can get 5 pounds (2.3 kilograms) of it for about twenty dollars, and that's enough to make around fifty bars of soap. You'll also want to purchase different colors of soap dyes. To really make your soap stand out, buy small plastic trinkets with fun shapes. These will go inside your bars of soap.

Make your soap in a kitchen with a trusted adult's supervision. First, lightly spray the inside of the plastic molds with cooking spray.

Then pour some glycerin soap into a measuring cup. Melt the soap in a microwave until it's all liquid—usually fifteen to thirty seconds. But stop before the soap begins to boil. You may need an adult to help you take the soap out of the microwave, because the measuring cup will be dangerously hot. If you have an adult's permission to handle the soap on your own, wear protective mitts.

Next, add a few drops of dye. Then stir the soap with a Popsicle stick. Carefully pour the soap into the molds, filling them about one-third of the way to the top. You'll have to work fast here because the soap hardens quickly.

Wait twenty minutes, and then drop a trinket into each mold. Melt and color some more soap. You can use the same coloring as before or mix things up with a different dye. Then pour the liquid soap onto the trinkets in each mold, covering the trinkets completely.

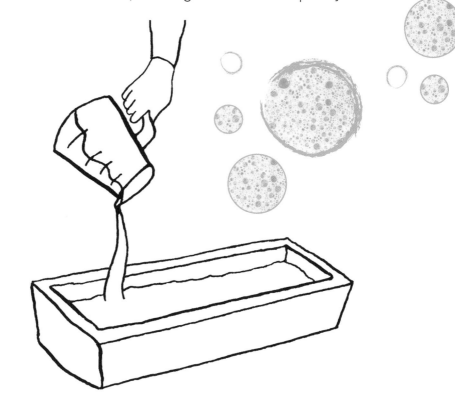

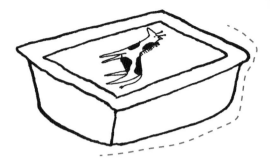

Two hours later, your soap should be cool to the touch. Dump it out of the mold, and wrap it in paper or plastic wrap. For an added touch, slip a homemade label in with the soap. This can be a colorful, neatly cut piece of paper. It should include the name of your business and tell customers how they can buy more from you.

After that, all that's left is the cleanup. Luckily, that's easy. Just rinse your molds with water, and let any leftover soap take care of the rest.

When it comes to soap, just about everyone is a potential customer. The trick is getting people to find your product. Set up tables at local garage sales or craft fairs. And send home free samples with your classmates. Include a small card or flyer with information about how their families can order more. As you spread the word, your business will grow!

CUSTOM NOTEBOOKS

Our world is full of smartphones, laptops, and tablet computers. But people still sometimes write the old-fashioned way: with paper and pencil. If you start a business selling custom notebooks, that paper could come from you.

Ask yourself, "If I make custom notebooks, who will buy them?" Will your friends and classmates need notebooks for school? What about artists who might use your notebooks for sketching? Can you sell to people who keep journals or enjoy creative writing? Will you appeal to busy adults who write to-do lists? If you can think of a good number of potential customers, then your business is worth a try.

First, gather supplies. For each notebook, get ten to twenty sheets of blank printer paper. Also choose a page of thick, colorful card stock for the cover. Your cover paper is what will grab customers' attention. Look online or at a local craft store to find paper with interesting patterns—or, better yet, add your own decorative touches to your covers. Draw designs with permanent markers or paint. Or use stickers, glitter, or even pipe cleaners to add flair. Plan to use different types of cover paper to create a variety of notebooks. Along with the paper, you'll also need a scissors, a ruler, a needle, and some thread.

Carefully fold your cover page and each sheet of printer paper in half the short way. Then unfold your cover page and layer your blank sheets inside it. The centerfolds of the blank paper should line up with the crease in the center of the cover paper. This area is called the spine. Use the scissors or a needle to carefully poke three small holes into the spine, through all the paper. One hole should be in the center, one should be 3 inches (7.6 centimeters) above it, and one should be 3 inches below it.

String your needle with about 20 inches (51 cm) of thread. (You can also use string or ribbon for a more decorative look.) Push the needle through the center hole of the cover, and pull the thread about three-fourths of the way through. Pull the needle and thread back out through the top hole. Keep the thread tight, but make sure you don't pull any more thread through the center hole.

Push your needle through the center hole again and bring it back out through the bottom hole. This should leave you with two ends of thread. Tie them together in a neat bow. Then cut away any extra thread. Just like that, your beautiful notebook is finished.

It's going to take some practice to get it right, and you'll make some mistakes along the way. That's okay. Just be very picky about which notebooks you sell. Keep the mistakes for yourself, or give them away. Sell only the notebooks that are high in quality, and your customers will be satisfied.

Working Wisdom: Make More!

You don't have to limit yourself to selling a single product. Many supplies, such as scrapbooking materials, can be used to make or decorate a variety of items. For instance, while you're making your own notebooks, why not create other paper products too? Bookmarks and note cards are fun and simple. And you can design them any way you want! Use light-colored card stock, and decorate the fronts.

A common size for bookmarks is 2 inches (5 cm) by 6 inches (15 cm). For a protective finishing touch, get them laminated at an office supply store. Or carefully cover each side with a smooth layer of clear packing tape.

Note cards are often 5 inches (13 cm) by 7 inches (18 cm) when folded. When you've finished your decorating, tie a stack together with ribbon or put them in a small gift box. You may want to buy and decorate envelopes to include with the note cards.

CUSTOM PHONE CASES

Do you want to make and sell something that's cool, trendy, and on the cutting edge of technology? Then consider going into business creating custom cases for cell phones.

The process is simple, but it leaves plenty of room for creativity. You can make designs on the computer, draw them by hand, or use your cut-and-paste skills to make scrapbook-like decorations.

If you want to start small, choose only one design. Perhaps you can create a case themed around your school mascot or a local attraction. If you'd like your product to make a bigger splash, put together as many ideas as you dare. You'll need to buy supplies to finish your work. But the more you can do up front—before spending any money—the smoother your process will be.

Show off your ideas to a few trusted friends and adults. Get their feedback. If everyone loves the designs, you're off to a great start. If no one likes them but you, try something different.

When you know what design materials you need, it's time to invest some money. Clear plastic cell phone cases should be at the top of your shopping list. These typically cost less than two dollars per case, and you can find them at cell phone stores, department stores, and online. You may want cases for the newest phone models. But if most of your potential customers use older phones, get cases for those models instead.

Along with the cases, you need a pencil, scissors, clear-drying adhesive (such as rubber cement), and your design supplies. Depending on your budget, you might buy anything from colorful printer paper to fancy adhesive decorations.

Set one of the cases you bought on a sheet of paper and trace around it. (Keep in mind that you'll have to trim the edges of your paper to make it fit inside the case.) Mark the spots where any openings need to be, such as a hole for the camera. Then have a blast creating your design.

Once that's finished, carefully cut out your design so it fits inside the case. Double-check that you've added all the necessary holes too. Next, lightly cover the side you designed with adhesive and slowly press it into the case. When you're finished, your design should show through the back of the case. Allow it to dry for up to two full days. After that, it'll be ready to go!

Use one of your cases on your own phone as a model. Show it off whenever you get the chance. And carry a few extra cases with you. If you see friends or classmates with coverless phones, let them know that you create custom cases. You just might make a sale.

Other places where your covers will get noticed include craft fairs and garage sales. Set up a table, and display your merchandise. Consider that some cell phone cases are priced at more than twenty dollars. If your cases look good and cost less, they're likely to sell. And you're likely to earn lots of money!

JEWELRY

You probably know the basics of jewelry making. Grab a string; slide some beads onto it; and tie it around your neck, wrist, or ankle. But with a little more thought and effort, you could turn this simple craft into a profit maker!

The key to success is to make jewelry that others find appealing. That starts by doing research. Visit stores. Browse catalogs and magazines. What jewelry designs seem to be popular? What are celebrities wearing? What kinds of jewelry do you and other people your age tend to like?

While you're getting a feel for jewelry design, you can also work on your jewelry-making skills. Plenty of books, websites, and videos can teach you how to create a variety of different jewelry. And while you're researching, find out if there are any bead stores nearby. Many of them promote learning within the stores. For instance, some stores offer worktables that let you make jewelry while you're there. Employees can provide tips and suggestions. You can also experiment with different beads, gems, and other materials.

If you invest enough time up front, you'll gain a handle on what to make and how to make it. Then you're ready to make your own designs! Grab a pencil and some paper, and start drawing. You may want to re-create some of the jewelry you've seen. Or you might try mixing and matching elements from different pieces of popular jewelry. Once you get the hang of it, your creations may come entirely from your own imagination.

When your designs are ready, create a list of materials. Then take a big gulp, because it's time to invest some money in your business. It's okay to start small. Maybe you want to buy only enough materials to create a few pieces of jewelry. After all, you can always go back for more after your first few products sell. But some of the things you'll need include wires, chains, rings, clasps, beads, and gemstones. On top of that, you'll also need tools such as pliers, scissors, and wire cutters.

Your products could be a huge hit, but only if you promote them. The easiest way to advertise is to wear your own jewelry—and get a few friends to wear it too. Anytime the jewelry gets noticed, use the chance to talk about your business. Answer all compliments with "Thanks! I make and sell my own jewelry." Then be ready with a card or a flyer that has information about how to buy your jewelry. Carry some extra jewelry in your backpack, bag, or purse. You just might make a sale on the spot!

As with all products, price matters. If you want to keep your pricing simple, consider charging about three times the amount it costs to make a given piece. So if you spend three dollars on materials to create a pair of earrings, a fair price might be nine or ten dollars. Of course, always ask yourself, "Would I pay that much for this product?"

Once you get the hang of designing and making your own jewelry, you may find that you have some loyal customers. If people like your products, they'll keep coming back for more. So keep your creations fresh and new. Who knows? You might become the next big success in the jewelry industry.

Working Wisdom: Managing Money

Making products to sell almost always begins with an investment. You need to buy supplies. You might also need to spend money on advertising your products or reserving a spot at an event. So save up your allowance and any gift money that you receive. But what if that's not enough to get started?

Do you believe in your business plan? Are you confident that your products will sell? If so, consider borrowing some money to get your work off the ground. Can you get a loan from family members? Or perhaps a parent or a guardian will help you borrow money from a bank.

When you do borrow money, of course, you have to pay it back. And sooner or later, you'll need to buy more supplies too. So you should manage your money carefully. Keep track of your sales, and budget your profits. Before you spend your income on other things, be sure that you have enough to pay for your loan and for more supplies.

Art means different things to different people. Illustration, sculpture, and photography are just a few of the forms it can take. You probably have at least some art displayed in your home. You might even have artwork hanging from the walls in your bedroom. For most people, artwork is a form of decoration—and they're willing to pay for it. That means if you can make it, you can sell it.

Maybe you love to paint landscapes. Perhaps you sculpt tiny, collectible dragons. Whatever art form you choose to pursue, you'll need to put in plenty of hours to become a success. Create as many pieces of art as you can. Then pick your very best to sell. Customers will only pay for art that they truly like, so you want them to see your finest works.

If you're an artist, you probably have most of the supplies you need. If you enjoy painting, then chances are you own paints and canvases. If you specialize in photography, you likely have a camera. But to give your art the best chance to sell, you will need to display it nicely. And unless you're a sculptor, that means you'll have to invest in a few nice picture frames.

Selling artwork is tricky business. You can't just put up a stand in your driveway and expect people to stop. And it's hard to carry sellable art around in your backpack. So you need to take a different approach to finding customers. You can even make an event out of it: your very own art show. Find a public location that you can use, such as a community center, a school, your place of worship, or a local restaurant. With an adult's help, arrange to have an open house there, where guests can come and look at your work. Send out invitations to family, friends, and classmates, and let them know that the artwork will be for sale. (If you want, you can invite your entire community too. Announce the event in your local newspaper.) Then make it a fun and memorable day. Serve snacks, spend time talking to your visitors, and be ready to discuss each piece of art and what inspired you to create it.

You can also try to sell your art through local businesses. Along with a parent or a guardian, talk to any small gift shops in your area. See if they're willing to display and sell your work. Coffee shops and restaurants are also popular places to sell art. Sometimes they'll hang art that's for sale on their walls. Just keep in mind that when you sell your products in stores and restaurants, those places usually keep up to 50 percent of the money.

A final option is selling your artwork online. Plenty of websites allow artists to sell their work in online galleries. With a parent or a guardian's permission and help, you can check out these options. You may find yourself with a countrywide customer base!

However you choose to sell your art, be proud of what you do. Show it off. Donate it to places that will hang it on their walls. And enter your artwork into contests whenever possible. Whether you win or lose, it's another chance for people to see your work.

Working Wisdom: Sell It at a Craft Fair

Many areas have craft fairs going on throughout the year—especially in November and December. These events are designed to give customers a chance to buy homemade goods. Craft fairs bring in plenty of people who are looking to spend money, so they can be good places to sell your products.

Small craft fairs often charge less than fifty dollars to rent a spot. If you think you can earn more money than you'll lose by paying the fee, see if you can line up transportation and adult supervision for an event near you. It could be a great chance to get your work noticed, meet other artists, and make a profit.

SCRAPBOOK DESIGN

• • •

You don't have to be an artist to take photographs. People snap pictures to capture memories every day. But what do they do with those photos? About one-third of the country turns to scrapbooking. It's a fun and creative way to display pictures. And you can turn that hobby into a job. Plenty of people want scrapbooks but either don't have the time or don't have the talent. Many are willing to pay someone to do the work for them.

If you go into business as a scrapbook designer, your clients provide you with photographs and instructions. They might tell you exactly what they want on each page, or they might leave the design entirely up to you. Either way, your job is to create a certain number of scrapbook pages—or an entire scrapbook.

Before you begin, you'll need to invest in scrapbooking supplies. The bad news: these can get pretty expensive. The good news: you can factor the cost of the supplies into the rate you charge for your services. Once you snag some paying customers, they can reimburse you for materials you buy for their projects. But you won't get hired until you've perfected your scrapbooking skills. That means you'll have to foot the bill for an album full of blank pages, page protectors, and decorative paper. Other basics include glue, tape, scissors, rulers, pens, and markers. And that's only the beginning. Down the road, you can use your earnings to add to your scrapbooking toolbox. Everything from metallic charms to decorative bling to embossing powders can add pizazz to a project.

Potential clients will want to see samples of your work. So put together a portfolio. It should show off your best designs and scrapbooking techniques. Be very picky about what you put in your portfolio. Each page should be one of your very best.

With your portfolio finished, you're ready for the hard part: finding clients. Tell everyone you know about your new business. Some of your first customers might be relatives and neighbors. Get permission to hang flyers where busy families might go. Grocery stores, restaurants, and public libraries are all good options. You can also

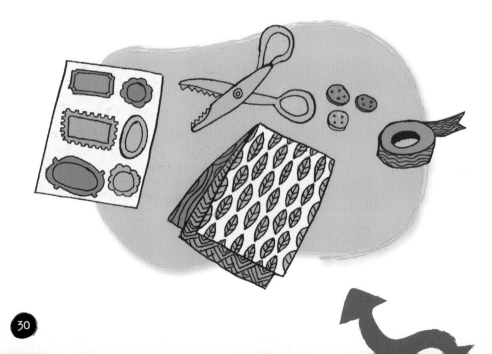

contact the craft stores and scrapbooking stores in your area. Perhaps they'll have a few advertising opportunities for you. They might also be able to point you toward potential customers.

A common practice for designers is to charge a set fee per page. How much does a typical page cost to decorate? How long does a page take to make? With that information, you can come up with a rate that will earn you a reasonable profit. Be ready to negotiate with your clients. Some might be willing to pay extra for fancier supplies or more elaborate projects.

For someone who loves the work, scrapbook design can be a dream job. You get to do something you enjoy. You get to help people share their most precious memories. And you get paid to do it!

SPIRIT FLAGS

Does your school have sports teams? Are there amateur athletics clubs in your community? Do people go to games to cheer on the local teams? Chances are you answered yes to all three questions. And if you did, you have a business opportunity. Cater to your community's sports fans by making and selling spirit flags.

Here's the plan. You'll make a few dozen flags in support of the most popular teams at your school or in your community. Any team that draws a crowd is fair game. In fact, if your school has other competitive groups—such as a marching band, a choir, or an academic team—you can target spectators at their events too. You'll bring your flags to competitions and sell them for a few dollars each. Your customers are already there, all in one place. So if your flags are high quality and don't cost too much, people will buy them. You might even start a trend, with fans waving your flags every time the team scores!

Before you launch this moneymaking scheme, make sure you can get permission to sell products at games. If you want to support a school team, speak with school officials. If you're rooting for a community league, contact the team's management and the venues where it plays.

When that's settled, get to work. Begin by choosing just one team to support with your flags. You can expand to other teams once you've mastered the basics of flag making. Make the flags any size you want, and design them however you'd like. Of course, the smaller and simpler your design, the smaller the expense. But the bigger and fancier the flags are, the more you can charge for them. Your challenge is to figure out what sells the best *and* makes you the most profit.

If you want to create something big, try a pennant. Pennants are sideways triangles that measure about 12 inches (30 cm) tall by 30 inches (76 cm) wide. If you're handy with scissors and glue, they're easy to create. But you'll need some supplies to assemble them.

Visit a fabric or craft store to buy material for your pennants. Wool and felt are good options. But for a sturdier product, make your flags out of interfacing—a heavy, stiff fabric. Look for materials in the colors of your chosen team. You'll also need felt and tacky glue, plus a 20-inch (51 cm) wooden rod. You also might use markers or acrylic paint for your design. And of course, you'll need the basics like a pencil, scissors, tape, and a ruler (or, better yet, a yardstick).

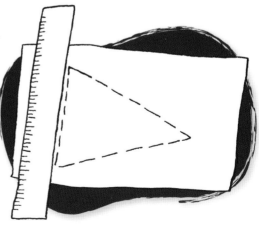

Your first step is to draw the 12-inch × 30-inch (30 cm × 76 cm) triangle on your fabric of choice. At the 12-inch end of the triangle, draw an attached rectangle that's

12 inches tall by 1 inch (2.5 cm) wide. You'll eventually attach this area to the wooden stick. Cut out the pennant, including the 12-inch × 1-inch area. Next, decorate your flag. The major design elements should be cut out of felt and glued to the pennant. This might include shapes or letters. Spell out the team's name, nickname, or slogan. Or feature a more general message, along the lines of "Go, team!" You can create patterns by printing them from a computer, or you can buy patterns at a craft store. Use a pencil to trace the patterns over your felt, and then carefully cut out your shapes. Position all your design elements exactly where you want them on the pennant. When everything is in place, glue each piece down. Then add extra decorative touches if there's room. Use a combination of markers, paints, and felts—whatever looks good and works best for you.

The last thing you'll need to do is attach your pennant to the wooden rod. Create a sleeve for the rod by folding the rectangular area in half. Glue along the top and side edge, but leave the bottom open. (If you find that you need to reinforce this area, try sewing or stapling it together.) When the pennant has dried, apply glue to the top 10 or 11 inches (25 to 28 cm) of the rod. Then slide the rod into the sleeve, and apply pressure until the rod sticks to the pennant.

When you're finished, you should have a beautiful and sturdy flag to wave. Create twenty or thirty more, and you'll be ready to make some serious money! You might have to experiment on a few test flags

before getting your design just right. But don't sell those practice ones—or any other flags that are poor in quality. If you only sell your best work, customers will quickly learn to expect top-of-the-line products from you.

With the right permissions, you should be able to set up a table near the concession stands—prime selling territory. But if you can't secure a booth, try wandering up and down the bleachers, selling flags to fans right from their seats. However you sell them, be proud of yourself every time you see those spirit flags waving!

PARTING WORDS

Running a successful business isn't just about talent. It takes hard work, planning, and patience. Even if you're not an artsy type, you can still create quality products that people will appreciate—and buy.

Think about the products that you can make. Then try your luck at selling them. It might be the start of an amazing opportunity.

$$$

NOW WHAT?

If you want to launch your business, begin with an action plan. To do that, grab a sheet of paper or hop onto a computer. Then answer these questions:

What skills will you need to practice before you start selling your products? What help will you need from adults, including family members?

How much money will it cost to buy your materials? How will you get that money? How will you pay it back?

Are there ongoing expenses after you begin? What are they? How will you manage your budget to pay for these expenses?

What are your goals? How many products do you hope to sell? How much do you want to make per project or per event?

What strategies will you use to sell products? Where and how will you advertise?

Will you need to file a tax return? By federal law, you must file a tax return if you earn more than a certain amount of money per year. Have an adult help you check IRS Publication 929 to find out what to do.

GLOSSARY

adhesive: a substance used for sticking materials together. When you work with crafts, you can paste your designs together with adhesives.

card stock: a type of paper that is thicker than normal paper. Card stock is used to make book covers, greeting cards, and bookmarks.

invest: to put money into a business with hopes of gaining even more money back. To start your new business, you might need to invest money into it.

laminate: to cover an object with a protective material, such as plastic. If you laminate paper, it becomes sturdier.

portfolio: a collected set of artwork or designs that show off a person's talent. You can show your portfolio to potential clients, so they know you're good at what you do.

profit: money gained after costs are subtracted from total earnings. Your total earnings from selling lemonade, minus the cost of the supplies, will be your profit.

unit cost: the amount one item costs to make. If you spend ten dollars to make ten items, your unit cost is one dollar.

FURTHER INFORMATION

Alex's Lemonade Stand Foundation for Childhood Cancer
http://www.alexslemonade.org
Get tips for running a successful lemonade stand, and find out how you can
link your business to a charitable cause.

Bernstein, Daryl. *Better Than a Lemonade Stand! Small Business Ideas
for Kids.* New York: Aladdin, 2012.
This fun guide is packed with creative ideas that show how to launch a
business with little or no start-up costs.

Hagler, Gina. *Money-Making Opportunities for Teens Who Are Artistic.*
New York: Rosen Publishing, 2014. Learn about different ways to make
money if you have artistic talent.

Jacobson, Ryan. *Get a Job Helping Others.* Minneapolis: Lerner
Publications, 2015. Interested in starting a business but not feeling crafty?
Check out this book for other ways to earn money.

Teaching Kids Business
http://www.teachingkidsbusiness.com
Visit this page for a program that will help you prepare for your new business.

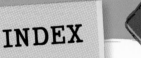

INDEX

PHOTO ACKNOWLEDGMENTS

The images in this book are used with the permission of: © evaschmidt/
Shutterstock.com, pp. 2, 23 (pliers); © Kladej/Shutterstock.com, pp.
2, 4, 23, 25 (beads); © Viktoriia Kulish/Hemera/Thinkstock, pp. 2, 29
(glitter); © Mike Flippo/Shutterstock.com, pp. 3, 34 (flags); © Andrey
Khritin/iStock/Thinkstock, pp. 4, 6, 8 (lemon slice); © Ruth Black/iStock/
Thinkstock, p. 4 (cupcake); © Nattika/Shutterstock.com, p. 5 (soap);
© CoolKengzz/Shutterstock.com, pp. 5, 14, 15, 16 (foam); © mamadela/
iStock/Thinkstock, pp. 5, 26, 27 (paint and brushes); © Anton Ignatenco/
iStock/Thinkstock, pp. 6, 8, 9 (lemon);© Wavebreakmedia Ltd/Thinkstock,
pp. 10, 12, 13 (cookie); © Kim DeClaire/iStock/Thinkstock, pp. 11, 13
(spoon); © mertcan/Shutterstock.com, p. 16 (soap); © pederk/iStock/
Thinkstock, pp. 17, 18 (needle and yarn); © BhubateT/Shutterstock.
com, p. 18 (yarn balls); © TashaNatasha/Shutterstock.com, p. 20
(thought bubbles); © Danylo Samiylenko/Shutterstock.com, p. 20
(phone cover); © Photodisc Royalty Free by Getty Images, p. 21 (pencil);
© TashaNatasha/Shutterstock.com, p. 22; © balabolka/Shutterstock.com,
p. 22 (phone covers); © Dino Osmic/iStock/Thinkstock, p. 28 (paint tubes);
© leedsn/Shutterstock.com, p. 29 (scissors); © Africa Studio/Shutterstock.
com, p. 31 (scrapbooking paper); © Andrey Kuzmin/Shutterstock.com,
p. 31 (photos).

Front Cover: © Africa Studio/Shutterstock.com (lemonade and brushes);
© Mike Flippo/Shutterstock.com (flags).

Main body text set in Avenir LT Std 11/18.
Typeface provided by Adobe Systems.